To ...Dad..

From ......Sarah..
Love,

WHY A

Daughter

NEEDS A

Dad

100 REASONS

Gregory E. Lang

with photographs by Janet Lankford-Moran

CUMBERLAND HOUSE

Published by Cumberland House, an imprint of Sourcebooks, Inc.
P.O. Box 4410, Naperville, Illinois 60567–4410
(630) 961–3900 Fax: (630) 961–2168
www.sourcebooks.com

Printed and bound in the United States of America.
BG 10 9 8 7 6 5 4 3 2

TO BECKY—THANK YOU

· INTRODUCTION ·

I WAS BORN INTO a loving family. My family is the kind that embraces you, nurtures you, and loves you immeasurably. For me, the most anticipated event of the year is our reunion at Thanksgiving, a tradition with a thirty-year history. I look forward to the sound of cheerful greetings, the warmth of hugs and firm handshakes, the comfort of kisses and familiar smells, and the retelling of stories of a Thanksgiving past, all of which rush toward me as soon as I set foot inside the front door. This love I have received shapes the love I give, and I hope it is evident at its best in my relationship with my daughter.

I have known from an early age that I wanted to be a father, and particularly the father of a daughter. My heart always melted when I held a baby girl, and I grew envious when I watched a toddler crawl onto her dad's lap to cuddle. I've been touched by women who spoke fondly of their fathers and moved by the grief of women who have lost their fathers. The special love shared between a daughter and father was something I very much wanted to experience for myself.

When my wife told me she was pregnant I was overjoyed. Something inside me told me that our child would be a girl. Throughout the pregnancy I referred to the baby as "she"—never "it"—and when we saw the first sonogram I insisted that it was obviously a girl, even though the doctor said it was too early to tell. I was in the delivery room when she arrived. The first person she looked at was me. I was smitten instantly.

After the delivery an exhausted mother slept while Meagan Katherine and I bonded. She slept on my shoulder, her face nestled under my chin. We spent her first night in the world together, asleep in a big recliner. Today, nearly twelve years later, Meagan still lays her head on my shoulder and turns her face into my neck. I still pull her close and make sure no harm comes to her.

Over the years Meagan and I have shared many special times together. We've had daddy-daughter dates, traveled, explored new subjects, and done sweet things for one another now and then. Sometimes we sit on the floor and look through the contents of the "Meagan Box," a cardboard box overstuffed with pictures, her artwork, keepsakes, and notes we have written to each other. In that box resides the reassuring evidence of our close relationship. Her mother and I divorced years ago, and Meagan lives with me half of the time. During the weeks that she is with her mother, I go to that box often. For a long time I have wanted to capture those memories and put them together in some form to give to Meagan, to reassure her that when we are not together I think of her and I love her.

I knew from the start that my relationship with Meagan would be a changing one. I knew, and people told me, that one day she would be a little less affectionate, more interested in friends, and less entertained by me, and that she might even find me embarrassing. It has surely come to pass. Now when I take her to school, she kisses me good-bye, and never on the lips, *before* we leave the house. I must turn off my music the moment the car enters school territory. I am to keep both hands on the wheel, my gaze fixed straight ahead. I may wave at other parents, but only if they wave first. If I must say, "I love you," it is to be nearly whispered, and never if the car door is open. Sometimes I go to the Meagan Box to reassure myself.

When I first began this book, my intention was to create a different kind of how-to book, a book daughters could give to their fathers to tell them what they wanted from them. I sat and thought about what my daughter and I had done together. I thought about what kinds of experiences my father had shared with my sister, and my uncles with my cousins. I asked Meagan for ideas, and I turned to the book of Proverbs for inspiration. Then I wrote it all down. The first time I read what I had written, I saw a list of what a daughter might ask her father to do for her (just as I had planned). The second time I read it, I saw a list of all that I hope to do for my daughter. The third time I read it, I saw myself telling Meagan that she would change but never outgrow me. When I read it the fourth time, I knew I was holding the Meagan Box.

Happy with the text, I set out to find a photographer. I did not know Janet Lankford-Moran when I began this book. I literally picked her at random out of the newspaper where she appeared in an article about a local art college. I sent her my manuscript and asked her to work with me. We met one afternoon to talk business. During this meeting she told me her personal story. She was raised by her single father beginning in her early childhood. She shared with me that she could see herself and her father in much of the manuscript. I knew then that we had to complete this book together. I did not have to tell Janet what I wanted the photographs to convey. She knew herself, perhaps even better than I.

With this book Janet and I hope to inspire new as well as experienced fathers to embrace the challenging role they play in their daughters' lives, to give them the love, nurture, and support they seek, and to cherish that which is reciprocated in kind. With this book I tell my child how very irreplaceably important she is to me. With this book I comfort and reassure myself that I will always have the pleasure and honor of being in her life. I love you, Meagan Katherine.

WHY A

Daughter

NEEDS A

Dad

A

Daughter

· *Needs a* ·

DAD

....

to learn that when he says it will
be okay soon, it will.

....

to share in her joys and triumphs as
she grows up and grows older.

A Daughter
· Needs a ·
DAD

···

who will make sacrifices
so she will not have to sacrifice.

···

A
Daughter
· Needs a ·
DAD

WHO WILL LAUGH WITH HER
AT ALL THE RIGHT TIMES.

· ·

to teach her that her value as a person
is more than the way she looks.

· ·

WHO WILL NOT PUNISH HER FOR
HER MISTAKES, BUT HELP HER
LEARN FROM THEM.

A

Daughter

· *Needs a* ·

DAD

WHO WILL ALWAYS HAVE TIME TO
GIVE HER HUGS AND KISSES.

·

*who does not mind when she steps
on his shoes while dancing.*

·

WHO WILL ALWAYS MAKE SURE
SHE HAS A PLACE TO COME HOME TO.

A

Daughter

· *Needs a* ·

DAD

who will never think she is
too old to need him.

A

Daughter

· Needs a ·

DAD

TO TEACH HER TO BELIEVE THAT SHE
DESERVES TO BE TREATED WELL.

*to teach her to accept the
differences in others.*

TO TEACH HER TO WEIGH THE
CONSEQUENCES OF HER ACTIONS AND
MAKE DECISIONS ACCORDINGLY.

A

Daughter

· *Needs a* ·

DAD

....

to make the family whole and complete.

....

A

Daughter

· *Needs a* ·

DAD

TO PROTECT HER FROM SCARY
NIGHTTIME CREATURES.

·

to answer the questions that
keep her awake at night.

·

TO PROTECT HER FROM
THUNDER AND LIGHTNING.

A

Daughter

· *Needs a* ·

DAD

· ·

so she will know what it is like
to be somebody's favorite.

· ·

A

Daughter

· *Needs a* ·

DAD

TO MAKE THE COMPLEX SIMPLE
AND THE PAINFUL BEARABLE.

·

to join her journey when she
is too afraid to walk alone.

·

TO TEACH HER THE MEANING OF
INTEGRITY, AND HOW TO AVOID
THE CROOKED PATH.

A

Daughter

· *Needs a* ·

DAD

· ·

to tell her truthfully that she
is the most beautiful of all.

· ·

A

Daughter

· *Needs a* ·

DAD

TO MAKE THE TOUGH DECISIONS
FOR HER UNTIL SHE IS ABLE TO
MAKE THEM FOR HERSELF.

·

*to teach her that forgiving is
a natural thing to do.*

·

TO TEACH HER THAT SHE CAN
FORGIVE MORE THAN ONCE.

A
Daughter
· *Needs a* ·
DAD

···

to teach her that family is
more important than work.

···

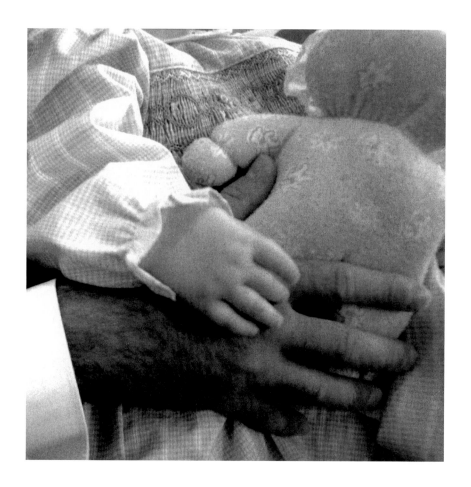

A

Daughter

· *Needs a* ·

DAD

to be the safe spot she can always turn to.

A
Daughter
· *Needs a* ·
DAD

....

to show her how it feels to be loved unselfishly.

....

A

Daughter

· *Needs a* ·

DAD

··

to be the standard against which
she will judge all men.

··

A

Daughter

· Needs a ·

DAD

TO TEACH HER THE DIFFERENCE
BETWEEN BEING FIRM AND
BEING STUBBORN.

*to teach her that she is
equal to her husband.*

TO TEACH HER THAT RESPECT IS TO BE
EARNED, AS HE HAS EARNED HERS.

A Daughter

· *Needs a* ·

DAD

TO LEARN WHAT SHE SHOULD EXPECT
FROM HER HUSBAND.

·

to teach her how to be responsible for others.

·

TO TEACH HER TO PRESERVE HER DIGNITY
DURING DIFFICULT TIMES.

·

to help her believe in herself as a parent,
and that in discipline there is hope.

A
Daughter
· Needs a ·
DAD

who will influence her life
even when he isn't with her.

A

Daughter

· Needs a ·

DAD

so that she will have at least one
hero who will not let her down.

A

Daughter

· Needs a ·

DAD

....

to tuck her in at night.

....

A

Daughter

· *Needs a* ·

DAD

....

to protect her when she is not
wise enough to protect herself.

....

A Daughter

· *Needs a* ·

DAD

TO TEACH HER TO BE HONEST
IN ALL HER DEALINGS.

·

to teach her patience and kindness.

·

TO TEACH HER WHEN TO BE FIRM
AND WHEN TO COMPROMISE.

·

to help her try again
whenever she fails.

A

Daughter

· Needs a ·

DAD

....

to help her take the risks
that will build her confidence.

....

A Daughter

· Needs a ·

DAD

....

to prepare her to persevere through hardship.

....

A

Daughter

· *Needs a* ·

DAD

··

who will let her know that while she
may not be the center of someone else's world,
she is the center of his.

··

A
Daughter

Needs a

DAD

TO GIVE HER THE GUIDANCE SHE
NEEDS AS SHE BEGINS TO RESOLVE
HER OWN TROUBLES.

·

*to pull her back when she is headed
in the wrong direction.*

·

TO THINK HIGHLY OF HER
WHEN NO ONE ELSE WILL.

·

to hold her as she cries.

A

Daughter

· Needs a ·

DAD

to be the history of her family
for her own children.

A

Daughter

· *Needs a* ·

DAD

to teach her what it means
to always be there.

A

Daughter

· Needs a ·

DAD

....

to teach her that a man's strength
is not the force of his hand or his voice,
but the kindness of his heart.

....

A

Daughter

· Needs a ·

DAD

TO TEACH HER TO RECOGNIZE
TRUTH AND REWARD IT.

·

*to teach her to recognize sincerity
and encourage it.*

·

TO TEACH HER ABOUT FAIRNESS.

·

to teach her to stand up for herself.

A
Daughter
· *Needs a* ·
DAD

....

to remind her of what she may not remember.

....

A

Daughter

· *Needs a* ·

DAD

....

to give her the gentle pushes
that help her grow.

....

A
Daughter
· *Needs a* ·
DAD

··

so that when no one else is there for her,
she can close her eyes and see him.

··

A

Daughter

· *Needs a* ·

DAD

....

to carry her just because she wants to be carried.

....

A

Daughter

· *Needs a* ·

DAD

....

to set a moral standard for her.

....

A

Daughter

· Needs a ·

DAD

....

to share with her the wisdom
she has not yet acquired.

....

A

Daughter

· Needs a ·

DAD

TO CALM HER WHEN SHE IS STRESSED
BY HER CHALLENGES.

. . . .

who teaches her she is important by
stopping what he is doing to watch her.

. . . .

TO GIVE HER A STRONG,
WILLFUL CHARACTER.

A

Daughter

· Needs a ·

DAD

to remind her of the comfort of
being held near and feeling secure.

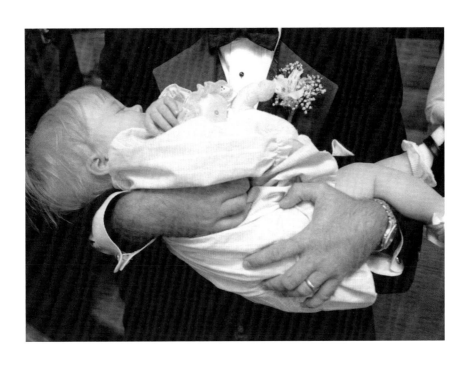

A

Daughter

· *Needs a* ·

DAD

· ·

to build a loving house on a foundation
of wisdom and understanding.

· ·

A

Daughter

· Needs a ·

DAD

TO HELP AROUND THE HOUSE SO
THAT HER MOTHER WILL HAVE TIME
TO SPEND WITH HER, TOO.

*to teach her that her role in a family
is greater than the work she does.*

TO HELP HER BECOME THE BEST
MOTHER SHE CAN BE.

A

Daughter

· *Needs a* ·

DAD

TO TEACH HER HOW THINGS WORK.

....

to show her how to fix
things for herself.

....

TO FIX HER FAVORITE THINGS.

A

Daughter

· *Needs a* ·

DAD

....

to teach her the importance of being a lady.

....

A

Daughter

· *Needs a* ·

DAD

....

who gives her refuge in a
home secured with faith.

....

A

Daughter

· Needs a ·

DAD

TO TEACH HER THAT IGNORANCE IS
NOT AN EXCUSE FOR ANYTHING.

·

*to teach her not to let pride get in
the way of discovering new things.*

·

TO TEACH HER TO EXPERIMENT FOR
THE SAKE OF TESTING HER OWN
ASSUMPTIONS.

·

*to teach her how to focus her mind
in the midst of distraction.*

A

Daughter

· Needs a ·

DAD

....

to teach her the joy of serving others.

....

A

Daughter

· *Needs a* ·

DAD

....

to show her that true love is unconditional.

....

A
Daughter
· Needs a ·
DAD

TO TELL HER ALL SHE NEEDS
TO KNOW ABOUT BOYS.

•

*to show her that all boys are
not like the one who hurt her.*

•

TO TEACH HER HOW TO
RECOGNIZE A GENTLEMAN.

A

Daughter

· Needs a ·

DAD

to teach her that loving her family is a priority.

A Daughter

Needs a

DAD

to teach her that a joyful heart is filled
with peace rather than deceit.

A
Daughter
· Needs a ·
DAD

....

to teach her when to be cautious.

....

A

Daughter

· Needs a ·

DAD

....

to teach her that men and women
can be good friends.

....

A

Daughter

· *Needs a* ·

DAD

TO TEACH HER WHAT KIND OF MAN
TO CHOOSE TO BE THE FATHER
OF HER CHILDREN.

*to stand with her on the day she
marries the man she hopes will be
just like her father.*

TO HELP HER RAISE HER CHILDREN
WITH STRONG FAMILY VALUES.

A

Daughter

· *Needs a* ·

DAD

....

to teach her to learn from her experiences.

....

A

Daughter

· *Needs a* ·

DAD

....

to help her find her way in life.

....

A

Daughter

· Needs a ·

DAD

TO SHOW HER THE BENEFITS
OF HARD WORK.

·

to teach her to spend responsibly, save
for a rainy day, and give with
a generous heart.

·

TO HELP HER FINISH HER WORK
WHEN SHE IS TOO WEARY TO
FINISH IT HERSELF.

A

Daughter

· *Needs a* ·

DAD

....

so she learns that men can be trustworthy.

....

A

Daughter

· *Needs a* ·

DAD

because without him she will have
less in her life than she deserves.

· ACKNOWLEDGMENTS ·

This book could not have been written without the support and generosity of many people. I offer a special thanks to the daughters and dads who shared their stories with me, who became my friends during this process, and who helped me find the heart of the matter, the profound and nearly endless reasons why daughters need their dads. I was deeply touched by the love I witnessed in the time I spent with you.

I also wish to thank my daughter, Meagan Katherine, and her friend Lauren Heusel, who helped me make sure this book had the right "girl touch," and the administration of Greater Atlanta Christian School, which helped me once more recruit families to participate in creating this book.

Finally, I wish to thank Ron Pitkin and the staff at Cumberland House, but especially my editor, Lisa Taylor. Lisa, in this fifth book we have completed together, I can truly say that you have added style to the books and made them better than I envisioned. May all my editors be so pleasant to work with. You have my deepest appreciation and warmest regards.

· TO CONTACT THE AUTHOR ·

Write in care of the publisher:
Gregory E. Lang c/o Sourcebooks, Inc.
P.O. Box 4410
Naperville, IL 60567-4410

Email the author or visit his website:
gregoryelang@gmail.com
www.gregoryelang.com